EO WRITES

Deep Calleth to Deep
Poetry & Prayers

First published by EO Writes 2025

Copyright © 2025 by EO Writes

All rights reserved. No part of this publication may be reproduced, stored or transmitted in any form or by any means, electronic, mechanical, photocopying, recording, scanning, or otherwise without written permission from the publisher. It is illegal to copy this book, post it to a website, or distribute it by any other means without permission.

EO Writes asserts the moral right to be identified as the author of this work.

First published by EO Writes 2025
Copyright © 2025 by EO Writes

It is illegal to copy this book, post it to a website, or distribute it by any other means without permission EO Writes asserts the moral right to be identified as the author of this work.

For permission requests, please address EO Writes.
For information, address: EO Writes lizzy@eowrites.com

Cover and interior designed by EO Writes.

All scripture quotations, unless otherwise shown, are taken from The King James Version, public domain.

First edition

First edition

This book was professionally typeset on Reedsy.
Find out more at reedsy.com

Contents

I Bride

1	The Bride is Awake	3
2	Big	4
3	The Great Shepherd	5
4	Break the Chains	6
5	Fresh Mercies	7
6	The Lord Keep Me	8
7	Ever Wondrous	9
8	The Great Exodus	10
9	Father & Daughter Dance	11
10	Heart Set Ablaze	12
11	My Plight	13
12	Sacrifice	14
13	Blessed	15
14	Sing Canary, Sing	16
15	Box of Treasures	17
16	True Joy	18
17	Needs Met	19
18	Ekklesia	20
19	Sunflower	21
20	Divine Explosion	22
21	Whom Shall I Fear?	23

22	New Season	24
23	A New Day is Upon Us	25
24	Heart Position	26
25	Flirtation Can Lead to a Dangerous Attraction	27
26	Risen	28
27	A Woman That Fears the Lord	29
28	Changing of the Guard	30

II   Kings & Queens

29	Watch Them Fall	33
30	Crowns	34
31	Queen of Babylon	35
32	Inheritance	36
33	King Nebuchadnezzar	37
34	Egypt	38
35	Rock of Ages	40
36	The Once Mighty Have Fallen	41
37	Desolation to Babylon	42

III   Prayers

38	Psalm 1	45
39	Help Us Watch	46
40	Our Daily Bread	47
41	Shepherd's Tree	48
42	About You	49
43	Mountains of Influence	50
44	A New Beginning	51
45	Come Home (song)	53

IV Occupations

46 What is a Writer?   57
47 What is An Illustrator?   58
48 Father's Are Special   59
49 A Mother's Purse   60

V Letters

50 Remove the Weights   65

About the Author   66
Also by EO Writes   68

I

Bride

One

The Bride is Awake

Awake, awake put on thy strength.
For it is time to come awake as God
causes a quake as the bride comes awake.

Two

Big

Who is big upon the land? Who is dressed oh, so grand?
Who is equipped from power on high ever reaching for the sky?
Her beauty no one can deny.
For she is the apple of His eye!
The Bride!

Three

The Great Shepherd

Ever working, ever true.
He is forever for you.
He doesn't sleep for he has sheep to keep.
When he confronts a foe he will not stop until they let go.
For Jesus is greater than any foe and he will not let us go.

Four

Break the Chains

Awake, awake it's time to break the chains
for there is much at stake.
A nation, a family, and a board game called monopoly.

Five

Fresh Mercies

Why go about mourning?
For his mercies are new each morning.
Give Him some praise and you will be amazed
by his glorious grace.

Six

The Lord Keep Me

You keep me in the night.
You keep me in the day.
You keep me even on a holiday.
You always know what to do and say.
For you Lord have paved my way.
And will see me to that great and glorious day.[1]

---

[1] ... and the glory of the LORD shall be revealed, and all flesh shall see it together: for the mouth of the LORD hath spoken it.
Isaiah 40:5

Seven

Ever Wondrous

Ever wondrous,
forever true
God Almighty is for you.
He sent his Son from above so that
you would know of his vast love.
He looked long ago and saw a
child empty of his wondrous glow.
He reached out as far as his hands would go
to give the biggest bear hug the world will ever know.

Eight

The Great Exodus

By receiving his hand we are welcomed into the promise land.
A land of plenty where we won't be running on empty.
As God supplies our every need and blesses
those who truly believe.
In hope that others will receive and be a part
of his family.

Nine

Father & Daughter Dance

Father and daughter danced along.
You could see he was sturdy.
You could tell they were strong.
No matter what the years brought along.
Even to the end they danced to their own song.
They danced steady and strong.

Dance, dance along.
Dance so beautifully, steady and strong.
No matter what life may bring along.
They danced steady and strong.

I can hear the Father say well done as the dancers
came in to greet the Son.
So dance my child, dance along.

Ten

Heart Set Ablaze

The word of the Lord was in my heart
setting it ablaze, setting it apart.
For I am not sure where to start
but I know there is a burning flame
in my heart.
I knew from the start that I was set apart
and I am now awaiting the fulfillment
of God's heart.
When he will impart what's in my heart
to those who are open to his heart.

Eleven

My Plight

You know my plight in this life.
You know where I am at and where I have been.
You know my beginning and my end and with that
I can confidently say amen!

Twelve

Sacrifice

A cold morning in the fall gave a chill to all.
But to one warmth came
as the Son shined over her once again.
A sacrifice of a time long past has now
received a second glance.
A sacrifice to honor the one and only Son
and it is now known what was done.
Letting go is hard to do but can be done when you say I do.
As the one and the past parted ways God received all the praise.

Thirteen

Blessed

Never mess with what God calls blessed.
For though sometimes we may look like a mess
God loves us and sends us his best.

Fourteen

Sing Canary, Sing

You have a song to sing!
A "canary" in the west wing.
Sing it loud.
Sing it clear.
Sing it so that all can hear
the message they so desperately need to hear-
do not fear, God is here!

Fifteen

Box of Treasures

A box of treasures
with perfect measures,
and significant endeavors
of equal matters.

Sixteen

True Joy

True joy isn't about things going our way.
For things gotten this way rarely stay.
It's about pleasing the Father along the way
and finding the pleasure of walking with him
each and every day.

Seventeen

Needs Met

Needs are met,
blessings galore
at the front door
when you are trusting the Lord.

Eighteen

Ekklesia

Who is this that I see?
It's the Ekklesia coming 1,2,3…
They were sent from Him
to bring about a great change from within.
With his hands and a high lifted chin,
they will rebuild for Him
using the tools that he gave them.

Nineteen

Sunflower

We as followers of Christ need
to stand tall for all to see.
Looking to Him for all we need.
Ever pointing up for all to see
that it's only by Him that we truly receive.

Twenty

Divine Explosion

The LORD is my light and my salvation,
my heart and my revelation.
With Him I have much consolation.
For he never ceases to be part of the equation
to my intervention.
Therefore stirring in my heart a revolution
of a divine explosion.

Twenty-One

Whom Shall I Fear?

Whom shall I fear when God is near?
Ever present, ever true.
He is always here for you.
Never doubt, never fear
for God will always be near to you.

Twenty-Two

New Season

New friends.
New places.
New graces.
Ah new faces…

Twenty-Three

A New Day is Upon Us

A new day.
A new view.
Out with the old,
in with the new.
As I bid everyone a farewell and adieu
as I embrace the new.[2]

---

[2] Therefore if any man be in Christ, he is a new creature: old things are passed away; behold, all things are become new. 2 Corinthians 5:17 KJV

All Things New by Kimberly & Alberto Rivera

Twenty-Four

Heart Position

Meditating upon your law night and day.
Seeking out what you have to say.
Leaning more into your heart with each passing day.
Knowing come what may everything is going to be okay.
For you are the one I am trusting with each of my days.

Twenty-Five

Flirtation Can Lead to a Dangerous Attraction

As young children it is innocent fun
but as adults you can become undone.[3]

---

[3] Based on the song, "A Tisket, A Tasket." A song about responsibility and flirtation. The song warns people of all ages to take good care of their belongings. For if you are careless, someone else may take them from you. You risk losing everything when you play. What was harmless as children can cause great loss as adults.

Twenty-Six

Risen

Why do you seek the living among the dead?
He has risen just like he said.

Twenty-Seven

A Woman That Fears the Lord

Charm is deceitful,
beauty is vain,
but a woman that fears the Lord,
she's ain't playing!

Twenty-Eight

Changing of the Guard

You Lord are changing the scenery to fit your itinerary.
The changing of the guard is coming into sight
to show the world what is wrong and what is right
and with thou's watchful eye they will make all thing's right.

II

Kings & Queens

Twenty-Nine

Watch Them Fall

Come one,
Come all,
watch them all fall.
For the greatest show of all
is about to expose them all.
The butcher, the baker, the candlestick maker.
All of those who came against their Creator.
In hopes that they would be greater
and they would control everything to the equator.

Thirty

Crowns

The wicked will not have a part.
Not a penny, not a dime, not even a tart.
For they thought with all their heart
they could have the crowns of those
who have been set apart.
God laughs at the sight for he knows
about the dynamite
that will cause the wicked's plans to ignite.

Thirty-One

Queen of Babylon

On the ground sat a crown
of one that fell down.
Now she no longer sits up high
with her scepter reaching the sky.
For she thought she was greater than I
but I AM the one who made the sky
and I AM the Most High.

Thirty-Two

Inheritance

The wicked will not have a part
of what God has promised in his heart.
His children big and small will fulfill His call.
He has promised them an inheritance
from his Son.
Just look at Psalm 51, and see what God has done.
For the turning of the tide has begun.

Thirty-Three

King Nebuchadnezzar

Nebuchadnezzar a King of old
made a statue forged in gold
whose height was even told.
He placed it before men and women long ago,
great and small and cast a decree before them all.
When the music notes fall then down on bended knee-all!
Yet there were three that would not bend for they were
dedicated to the great I AM!
And though he threw them in the fire and turned the furnace
up a notch or so higher
the Son of God brought them up even higher.
For obedience is what he requires!
Deliverance was what transpired as he delivered them from the
fire!

Thirty-Four

Egypt

The idols were upon the beasts,
a heavy load they continued to increase.
The carriages carrying a heavy load
to a way that was untold.
Soon the weary beasts gave way
to the increase of the day.
Which in turn caused the people to yield
their carriages, their idols to the fields.
Now free to run once more

they gave a shout to the LORD![4]

---

[4] Bel boweth down, Nebo stoopeth, their idols were upon the beasts, and upon the cattle: your carriages were heavy loaden; they are a burden to the weary beast.
Isaiah 46:1

If the Son therefore shall make you free, ye shall be free indeed.
John 8:36

Thirty-Five

Rock of Ages

Bel boweth down, Nebo stoopeth and fell down.
their idols-their crowns were nowhere to be found.
For they had lost all ground
as God's army had touched the ground.
And now a new battle rages, one of the ages,
one whose General is the Rock of all Ages.
He is turning the pages of a book that was written for all ages.

Thirty-Six

The Once Mighty Have Fallen

Come one, come all.
Watch them all fall.
Fall to the left, fall to the right.
For they did not fear that which was right.
They are NOW going to GIVE UP this fight.

Thirty-Seven

Desolation to Babylon

Declare ye among the nations
of a great desolation
to the Babylon manifestation!
For there is now a clear revelation
that we are entering the golden revolution
and a renewal of the constitution.
A declaration, and an emancipation
of a great global expansion
of God's illumination upon the nations.
Causing a global realization
of the emancipation from the God of all creation.

III

Prayers

Thirty-Eight

Psalm 1

As I pray Psalm 1 over my day.
I ask you Lord for your strength come what may.
May I think upon you and what you have to say.
Including you in every intricate part of my day.
May I be able to say at the end of the day
the Lord knoweth my way.

Thirty-Nine

Help Us Watch

Help us watch what we say.
Help us watch what we do.
Keeping our spirit's ever fresh
and free to serve you the one who is true.

Forty

Our Daily Bread

Lord,
Help us discern
wherever we go,
who are friends,
and who are foes.
That we may know in whom to share our heart
with and whom the answer is clearly no![5]

---

[5] Give us this day our daily bread. Matthew 6:11
Keep thy heart with all diligence; for out of it are the issues of life. Proverbs 4:23

Forty-One

Shepherd's Tree

Lord,
May I be like a Shepherd's tree
whose roots go down deep in thee.[6]

---

[6] A Shepherd's Tree has roots that reach the depths of 223 feet -deepest known root structure in the world.

Forty-Two

About You

In everything I say and do
may it be about you.
This is the reality of a walk that is true.
That others would see you in all I do
and therefore desire to know you.

Forty-Three

Mountains of Influence

Lord,
Bring the seven mountains of influence to their knees.
for the least of these.
That God's anger would be appeased.
That there would be victories that would bring
great harmonies to the least of these.
Enabling them to go forth and honor thee.

Forty-Four

A New Beginning

Lord,
I wait for the break upon the eight
they tried to suffocate.
In which the land will quake
as God honors the eight.
To facilitate another date
to congregate.
A collaboration to a celebration
as there is a change in the situation

regarding the nation.[7]

---

[7] 8- as in new beginning

God was ushering in a new beginning in 2020, then the enemy interfered with the COVID agenda.

I thought it was interesting that God used the word "honorates" being that word is now obsolete. It is only recorded in the mid 1500's.

Those who collaborated together will fall together.

Numbers 16 The true leaders challenged

Who is on the Lord's side?

Exodus 32:26

The changing of the guard!

They tried to put out God's fire! Then I said, I will not make mention of him, nor speak anymore in his name. But his word was in mine heart like a burning fire shut up in my bones, and I was weary with forbearing, and I could not stay.

Roll call is coming. People chose sides in 2020. God is about to ask the question again, who is on the Lord's side!

Forty-Five

Come Home (song)

All you who are weary and laden with care.
The Father is calling, come home.
My child hear him.
My child beware.
The Father is calling, come home.
Come home, come home, oh come home.
The Father is calling, come home.
All you who are weary and laden with care.
The Father is calling, come home.
Hear the Father calling, come home.

IV

Occupations

Forty-Six

What is a Writer?

What is a writer you may ask
as though it's some daunting task.
A word here, a word there,
more words than two
telling a story or two
to all of you.
A hero, a villain, there just may be
a mathematician.
Adventure, a mystery, maybe some rhyming poetry.
Self help, or get help.
It just may involve a lesson or two.
The point is a story is a written gift just for a you.

Forty-Seven

What is An Illustrator?

What is an illustrator you may ask.
Someone who is assigned an unusual task.
Creating a character from a fantasy world
or a King from a story long foretold.
Maybe a griffin, an elf, or a gazelle or two.
There is always much for them to do.
For stories come to life with a illustration or two.
Don't forget to acknowledge the work that they do.

Forty-Eight

Father's Are Special

Father's are special, special indeed.
They are always quick to lend a hand,
when you are in need of a strong man.
Whether tired, sick, or blue
he knows just what to do with
three simple words, "I love you."

Forty-Nine

A Mother's Purse

A mother's purse is like a play that has been thoroughly rehearsed.
With each segment of time there's a need in mind.
Chapstick for when it's cold, a tissue to blow one's nose.
Needle and thread to fix a button or a quote from E.F. Hutton.
Breath mints for those stinky predicaments and just maybe a small instrument.
Activity books galore for those times when you are just plain bored.
Are you in need of something sweet? Look to mom she usually has some kind of treat.
It's no small feat, it may not be neat, but everyone knows a mom's purse is quite unique.

A Mother's Purse

V

Letters

Fifty

Remove the Weights

Remove the weights that I would be able to run.
That I would be able to fly.
Soar so high that I could touch the sky.
Signed,
The Apple of Your Eye[8]

---

[8] ... but they that wait upon the LORD shall renew their strength; they shall mount up with wings as eagles; they shall run, and not be weary; and they shall walk, and not faint. Isaiah 40:31

About the Author

EO Writes has been married for 27 years. She and her husband enjoy traveling throughout the United States on their Harley. Her passion is speaking truth through her art and writing. She hopes to get her children's book, Luna Goes Exploring, published in 2026.

"Never judge a book by its cover. What you find inside the pages might surprise you."
Note from the Author:
"A word fitly spoken is like apples of gold in pictures of silver." Proverbs 25:11
If you have enjoyed this book, would you consider reviewing it on Amazon.com?
Thank you!

You can connect with me on:
- https://eowrites.com
- https://www.linkedin.com/in/elizabetho
- https://truthsocial.com/@Lizzywrites

Subscribe to my newsletter:
- https://www.subscribepage.io/write4him

Also by EO Writes

For who hath despised the day of small things? For they shall rejoice, and shall see the plummet in the hand of Zerubbabel with those seven; they are the eyes of the Lord, which run to and fro through the whole earth.
Zechariah 4:10

Penned with Purpose
Penned with purpose is an accumulation of fifty poems that I have written over a couple of decades.

A Case of Mistaken Identity
"Have you ever felt like the entire world was against you? In a case of mistaken identity, Sadie feels this way as a court trial challenges her deserving of a happy ending.

Getting Unstuck: A Guide to Self Publishing

Are you looking for a guide to help you navigate the journey of self-publishing? Glean off of someone who has been there.

www.ingramcontent.com/pod-product-compliance
Lightning Source LLC
Chambersburg PA
CBHW060423050426
42449CB00009B/2102